10

D1460014

Thanks to Marie-Dominique de Teneuille,
Béatrice Foulon, Frédérique Kartouby,
Hugues Charreyron and Annick Duboscq

For Julian and Nelly

Translation
Isabel Ollivier
Design and layout
Chloé Bureau du Colombier ·
Photoengraving
I.G.S.
Printed by
Imprimerie Alençonnaise

Cover illustration:
Footballer, 1961

Marie Sellier

My Little Picasso

Réunion
des Musées
Nationaux

There is a funny place in Paris

called the Salty Hotel.

It is not really a hotel,

but it is full all year round.

A very special visitor has moved in.

You already know him.

His name's Picasso.

6

The Hôtel Salé is his museum.

Come in and have a look!

There are weird paintings.

There are wonderful sculptures!

There is something of everything,

Something to suit all tastes!

there is... a bull's head

Did Picasso ride a bike?

We don't know, but he used a bike

to make the head of a bull.

A worn leather saddle,

rusty old handlebars...

And, hey presto!

A fighting bull ready for the ring!

But Picasso would really have loved

to turn back the clock,

toss the bull out the window,

and watch one boy seize the handlebars,

and another leap on the seat.

And see the bull turn into a bike again.

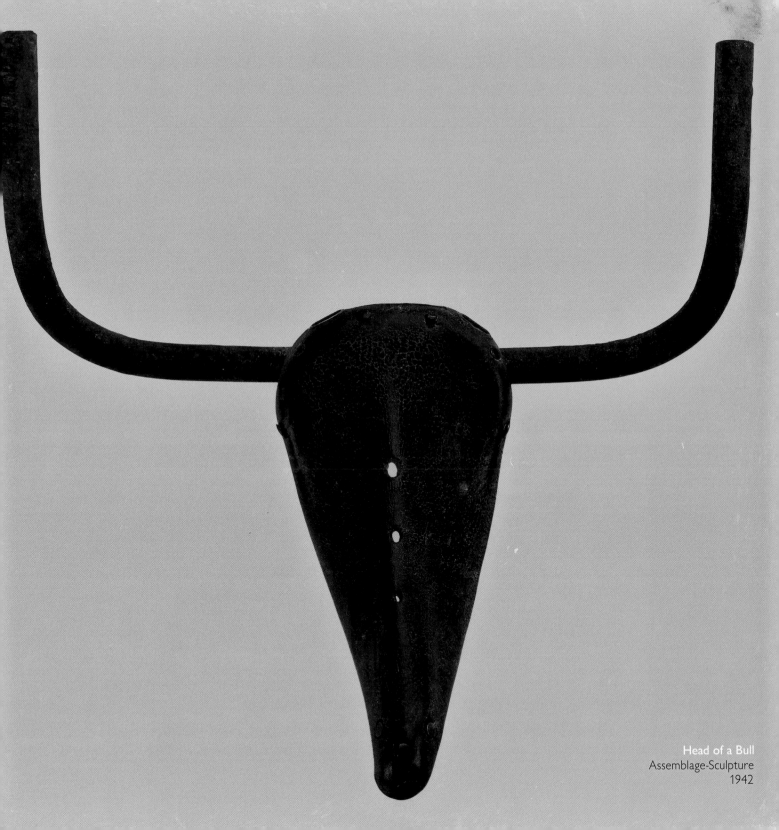

Head of a Bull
Assemblage-Sculpture
1942

there is... Picasso at twenty five

That's me, Picasso.

I'm not very tall but I'm sturdy.

I have painted myself bare-chested

and square-shouldered with a thick neck

strong enough to carry

a head twice as big as mine.

Pink against a grey background,

I look like a painted wooden statue.

My black eyes take everything in

and noises flood into my big ears.

I am just twenty five, but I already know

I will make a name for myself.

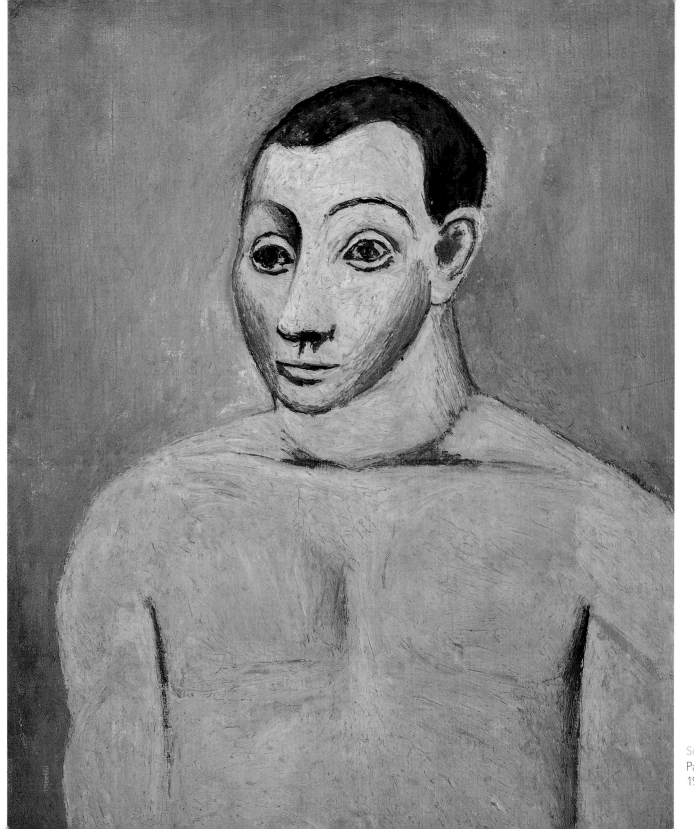

Self-portrait
Painting
1906

there is... a redskin mother and child

"Oh!" says the pop-eyed redskin boy.

"Well I never!" exclaims the mummy

with a bun, stifling a cry.

How astonished they look,

the hairless boy

and his blue-eyed mother.

What are they looking at?

Hah! That is Picasso's secret.

But if they turned round

they would see

that the woodland spirits

had slipped in among the trees.

Mother and Child
Painting
Summer 1907

there is... Olga in a silk dress

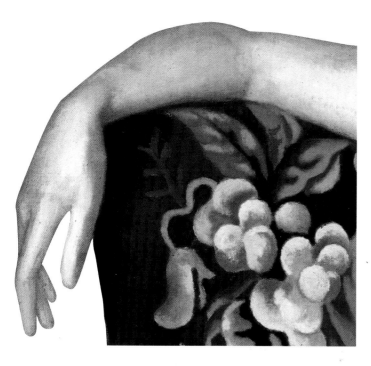

Olga is very elegant,

but she looks a little vague

perched there,

goodness knows why,

on an unfinished chair.

Who is she anyway?

A Russian dancer!

She is Picasso's wife, too,

and Paulo's mummy.

Portrait of Olga
on a Chair
Painting
1918

there is... a three-year-old Harlequin

When your name's Paulo
and you are Picasso's son
you have to get dressed up
in a yellow-and-blue Harlequin suit
and stay as still as a mouse
while he paints you.
But Paulo has had enough:
"Hurry up, Dad, I want to go
and play! Come on, Dad,
I've got pins and needles!
Hurry up! I'm going anyway.
Too bad if you haven't done my feet!"
Picasso puts down his brush: "Paulo with no feet?
Ha, ha! There's a bright idea!"

Paulo
in a Harlequin
Costume
Painting
1924

there are... two giant ladies on the beach

Two hefty great giants,

running by the seaside.

Hefty but light-footed.

They are running hand in hand,

but their solid sea legs

scarcely skim the dull sand.

Where are they going, Mr Picasso?

Why are they reaching for the sky?

Perhaps they will leap in the air,

and float with the clouds above the sea

on a summery day at Dinard.

18

Two Women Running on the Beach
Painting
1922

there is... an orange swimmer

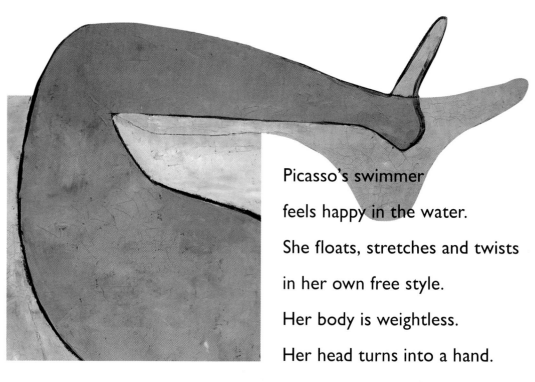

Picasso's swimmer
feels happy in the water.
She floats, stretches and twists
in her own free style.
Her body is weightless.
Her head turns into a hand.
Is that a nose?
Or a pointing finger
telling her to swim up
to the surface to breathe.

20

The Swimmer
Painting
1929

21

there is... Marie-Thérèse in an armchair

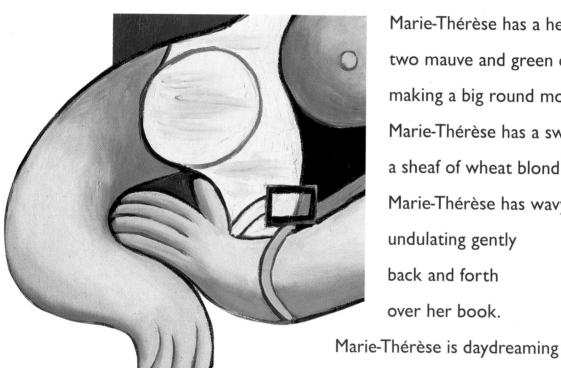

Marie-Thérèse has a heart-shaped face,

two mauve and green crescents

making a big round moon.

Marie-Thérèse has a sweep of golden hair,

a sheaf of wheat blond in the sun.

Marie-Thérèse has wavy arms and fingers

undulating gently

back and forth

over her book.

Marie-Thérèse is daydreaming

in a yellow and green striped chair.

Marie-Thérèse is Picasso's new love.

He paints her with circles and curves,

hollows, bumps and gentle caresses.

22

Reading
Painting
1932

there is... a dancing table

Picasso is a wizard.

He can make tables spin.

Under his brush,

   arabesques

     and round faces

      spring up

       between bowls and jars.

        The green apples boggle,

        the red cloth pokes out its tongue

        and the little table dances a jig

        on its three wooden legs.

        Who called it a still life?

Large Still Life with a Table
Painting
1931

there is ... Maya with her doll

Maya flicks her blond pigtails.

She rocks her doll then scolds her.

Maya is such a pretty little girl

that her daddy wants to paint her

from all sides at once.

Maya laughs

and jiggles,

full of life.

Not like her doll,

whose goody-goody face

will always be

the right way up.

Maya
with
her Doll
Painting
1938

there is... a cruel cat

Picasso's cat
has pounced on a bird
and torn its wing.
This cat is a killer.
The whites of its eyes are cruel
and its paws end
in sharp little knives.
Picasso's cat
does not have
a cat's head.
He looks like those men
who delight in making war.

Cat Catching a Bird
Painting
1939

there is... a bullfight on a plate

A terrific bullfight,

under the Spanish sun, olé!

The bull goes round and round

the ring and the bullfighter

joins him in a whirl of gold.

It's a fight to the death.

Picasso found bullfights

so thrilling that he painted

one on a plate.

Spanish Dish
Glazed Earthenware
1957

there is... Dora in rainbow colours

Picasso's heart wavers

between blonde Marie-Thérèse

and dark Dora.

Dora has a peach for a cheek

and a lemon for a chin.

Picasso has given her

one back-to-front green eye,

looking at a right-way-round red eye.

Dora's hands are tropical flowers

with blood red nails.

Dora is a prickly woman.

She has a bunch of knitting needles

in her heart.

Portrait of Dora Maar
Painting
1937

there is... Miss Catastrophe

To wake people up, Picasso painted portraits

every which way,

right way, wrong way,

crooked and all muddled up.

Miss Catastrophe

has come to pieces.

Her eyes have a life of their own,

her nose keeps a low profile,

her mouth is going backwards

her neck is playing at being a vase.

But she still likes to look pretty.

She has stuck a sprig of blue leaves

in her pancake hat.

Straw Hat
with Blue
Foliage
Painting
1936

there isn't... this picture

Here's the family at home.

Mummy, in green and white, is reading or resting

on the yellow sofa. That's Françoise,

Picasso's new wife. She has a low-cut dress

and her hair twisted in a knot.

The children are playing

on the red and blue rug,

Claude with his centipede train,

Paloma with her little tricycle.

This painting is not in Paris.

You have to go to Antibes, in the South

of France, if you want to see it.

Picasso painted so many pictures

that he has five museums all to himself!

Mother and Children Playing
Painting
1951

there is... a monkey-car

One little car right-side-up for the skull,

another little car upside-down for the jaw,

and there you have a classy monkey,

a Panhard-Renault cross.

But the baby monkey

is a frail thing,

no King Kong

with its ping pong head.

Picasso was a champion

at using old things.

Best not to leave toys about

when he was around!

Monkey and her Young
Sculpture-Assemblage
1951

there is... swan-necked Jacqueline

She has the almond eyes
of an Egyptian princess
and a longer neck
than a giraffe woman.
Her face is as white
as the white bands
on her yellow-striped dress.
Her hair is as black
as the black tiles
on the red and black floor.
Crouching silent and still,
waiting or watching over him,
Jacqueline is Picasso's last wife.

Jacqueline
with Folded Hands
Painting
1954

there is... a goat made of wood, straw and iron

Take an old wicker basket

for a nice round belly

because the nanny goat

is expecting kids.

Cut a big palm leaf for the back and brow.

Choose four sticks for the legs.

Tie on three twisted vines for the horns

and the goatee beard.

Add two milk jugs for the teats

and scrap iron wherever you please.

Plaster all over and listen carefully...

"Meee..." goes Picasso's goat.

The Goat
Original Plaster
1950

You will find the two giants,

the orange swimmer,

the dancing table and the others

at the Picasso Museum.

The museum is open every day,

except Tuesdays,

and for you it's free.

Photo credits:
Réunion des musées nationaux
Photographs by J. G. Berizzi, G. Blot,
B. Hatala, T. Le Mage/F. Raux, R. G. Ojeda

Registered: October 2002
ISBN 2-7118-4619-9
JC 50 4619